HOW TO TAKE THE CHAIR

Practical Handbook Series

Fcap 8vo Stiffened cloth

How to Conduct a Meeting *by* John Rigg

How to take the Chair *by* John Rigg

Watch Your English! *by* Harold Herd

Everybody's Guide to Punctuation *by* Harold Herd

A Simple Guide to Committee Procedure *by* E. O. Lambourn

How to Write Good Letters *by* Beryl Heitland

How to Conduct a Discussion Group *by* Beryl Heitland

HOW TO TAKE
THE CHAIR

by

JOHN RIGG

George Allen & Unwin Ltd
RUSKIN HOUSE MUSEUM STREET LONDON

FIRST IMPRESSION 1925
SECOND IMPRESSION 1925
THIRD IMPRESSION 1926
FOURTH IMPRESSION 1929
FIFTH IMPRESSION 1933
SIXTH IMPRESSION 1937
SEVENTH IMPRESSION 1944
EIGHTH IMPRESSION 1947
NINTH IMPRESSION 1948
TENTH IMPRESSION 1952
ELEVENTH IMPRESSION 1955
TWELFTH IMPRESSION 1959
THIRTEENTH IMPRESSION 1964
FOURTEENTH IMPRESSION 1970
FIFTEENTH IMPRESSION 1975

ISBN 0 04 380007 6

PRINTED IN GREAT BRITAIN BY
COMPTON PRINTING LTD
LONDON AND AYLESBURY

PREFACE

THIS little work, *How to take the Chair*, is intended to be a companion volume to the author's *How to Conduct a Meeting*. Like that book, it is based on Parliamentary Practice, but differs essentially in certain respects.

The present volume, for instance, does not contain a code of Standing Orders and Rules of Debate, as does *How to Conduct a Meeting*, but goes more into detail regarding matters stated generally in that publication. It also includes chapters on Miscellaneous Questions, Special Meetings, and Meetings of Companies.

The Miscellaneous Questions are questions concerning which the author's opinion has been sought by organized bodies that have adopted *How to Conduct a Meeting* as a *vade mecum*, and the chapter on Special Meetings is the result of a suggestion which came from a similar source; that on Meetings of Companies is inspired by a communication received from the publishers.

The success which has attended the publication of
How to Conduct a Meeting leads me to believe that
this companion volume will be found equally useful.
The two combined form, undoubtedly, a compre-
hensive treatise on the subject of meetings and
chairmanship.

JOHN RIGG.

CONTENTS

	PAGE
PREFACE	5
THE CHAIRMAN	9
PUBLIC MEETINGS	16
MEETINGS OF ORGANIZED BODIES	22
MOTIONS	24
AMENDMENTS	31
DIVISIONS	48
DEBATE	51
LIMITATION OF DEBATE	62
BREACHES OF ORDER	64
COMMITTEES	67
MISCELLANEOUS QUESTIONS	73
SPECIAL MEETINGS	79
COMPANY MEETINGS	81
INDEX	85

HOW TO TAKE THE CHAIR

THE CHAIRMAN

1. *What are the principal qualifications of a Chairman?*

The principal qualifications of a Chairman are tact, firmness, and impartiality.

2. *What should the Chairman be able to decide promptly?*

The Chairman should be able to decide promptly all questions of order or procedure.

3. *What is it necessary that the Chairman should understand in regard to himself?*

It is necessary that the Chairman should understand that, in order to control others, he should be able, at all times, to control himself.

4. *State the duties of a Chairman.*

It is the duty of the Chairman—

> To maintain order, and to see that due respect is paid to the Chair.

To listen attentively to everything that is said.

To confine the debate to the question under consideration.

To check undue and tiresome repetition.

To rule promptly on questions of order.

To demand the immediate withdrawal of offensive expressions, or expressions which may be regarded as likely to give offence.

To rule out of order all motions or proposed amendments which do not deal directly with the business then before the meeting.

To rule out of order all questions that do not comply with the rules of the organization.

To prevent a second speech.

To " state " and " put " questions to the meeting and declare, according to his opinion, whether " the ayes have it " or " the noes have it."

To declare the result of all divisions to the meeting and give a casting vote when necessary.

To " put " formal questions without amendment or debate.

5. *What is meant by " an offensive expression " ?*

" An offensive expression " means offensive words used with reference to another member, or words used that are considered objectionable by the Chairman.

"The imputation of bad motives; misrepresenting the language of another, or accusing him, in his turn, of misrepresentation; charging him with falsehood or deceit; or contemptuous or insulting language of any kind; all these are unparliamentary, and call for prompt interference." (See May's *Parliamentary Practice*, eleventh edition, pages 333–334.)

"The House of Commons will insist upon all offensive words being withdrawn, and upon an ample apology being made which shall satisfy both the House and the member to whom offence has been given." (May, page 335.)

6. *How should the Chairman deal with an offensive expression?*

If the offensive expression is not at once withdrawn when ordered by the Chairman, the Chairman should declare the offending member guilty of disorderly conduct, and require the meeting to deal with him.

A member of an organized body declared guilty of disorderly conduct may be punished, on resolution of the meeting—

(1) By being ejected from the meeting.

(2) By being suspended for a fixed period from attending meetings, or until he offers a satisfactory apology.

(3) By being fined.

Offenders of any kind may be ejected from a public meeting.

7. *Explain what may be done should the Chairman omit to notice an offensive expression, and state the Chairman's duty consequent thereon.*

On default of the Chairman a member may move, That the words be taken down. This is a motion that must be moved at once, or when the member using the words has resumed his seat, but before any other member addresses the Chair.

The member who desires words to be taken down must repeat the words to which he objects, and state them exactly as he conceives them to have been spoken.

When the motion has been moved the Chairman asks : " Is it the pleasure of the meeting that the words be taken down ? " Should the meeting decide that the words shall be taken down the Chairman gives the necessary order, or takes down the words himself. The words having been taken down, the offender is held to be guilty of disorderly conduct ; and the Chairman calls on some member to move a motion in regard to the offence.

8. *What should the Chairman explain (when necessary) in regard to motions and amendments ruled out of order ?*

When necessary, the Chairman should explain to the meeting that the motion or amendment then

ruled out of order may be in order at a subsequent
stage of the proceedings.

9. *What is meant by the expression : " The question
is " ?*

A question must be submitted to the meeting in
regard to each motion or amendment that has been
proposed and seconded, and it is for this reason that
the Chairman always uses the words " the question
is " when " stating " or " putting " a question to
the meeting.

10. *What is it of importance that the Chairman
should do when conducting business ?*

The Chairman should read and speak in clear and
firm tones. He should proceed with deliberation,
giving an opportunity for debate, or further debate,
should it be desired.

He should stand up when he speaks to the
meeting, and require others to be seated or remain
seated.

He must permit himself to be interrupted when
" putting " a question by any one desiring to continue
the debate, and resume the Chair in the meantime.

11. *Is it the duty of the Chairman to ask for
amendments to a motion, or to invite debate ?*

It is not the duty of the Chairman to ask for
amendments to the motion or invite debate ; but
he may do so if he deems it advisable.

12. *What is the rule ?*

The rule is that the Chairman shall "put" the question so soon as a member has resumed his seat, unless another member rises to address the meeting.

13. *What should the Chairman of an organized body do when he desires to debate a question or vote on a question ?*

When the Chairman of an organized body desires to debate a question or vote on a question, he should vacate the Chair after arranging the appointment of an Acting-Chairman, unless a Deputy-Chairman has been already appointed or elected.

When the Chairman desires to leave the Chair temporarily for any reason, and there is no Deputy- or Acting-Chairman, the Chairman may invite any member to take the Chair and preside during his temporary absence.

14. *Has the Chairman of a meeting the right to vote on questions " put " by himself as Chairman ?*

No. The Chairman has a casting-vote only. The Chairman of a Select Committee, or a Standing Committee (such as a Board or Committee of Management), has a deliberative as well as a casting-vote.

15. *Has the Chairman of a meeting power to adjourn the meeting at his own will and pleasure ?*

> *It has been held in the Law Courts of England*
> *that a Chairman has no power to adjourn a*

meeting because he disapproves of something that has been done or is being done. Should he do so, the Deputy-Chairman, or, in his absence, a person appointed by the meeting, may take the Chair and the business of the meeting be proceeded with.

If the members act in so disorderly a manner as to prevent the Chairman conducting the business properly, the Chairman may declare the meeting closed, and leave the Chair.

PUBLIC MEETINGS

16. *What is a public meeting ?*

A public meeting is a meeting called by a citizen, or any number of citizens, to discuss a question or questions of public interest.

It often happens that a meeting is called by an organized body, and the public are invited by advertisement to attend. Such a meeting is spoken of as a public meeting. It is not, however, in the true sense of the term, a public meeting, for it is controlled entirely by the officers of the organization. Strictly speaking, it is an open meeting of the organization— meaning a meeting of the organization open to the public.

17. *Describe the steps you would take to convene a public meeting, and the arrangements you would make for holding it.*

I would call the meeting by circular, or by distributing hand-bills, or by advertisement in the newspapers ; or I might employ all these methods.

I would also arrange for a personal canvass of people I specially desired to be present.

I would see that, in all notices in regard to the

meeting, the three most important matters were
clearly set forth—

(1) The place of meeting ;

(2) The day and date of the meeting ; and

(3) The hour at which the meeting is to commence.

On the day of the meeting, I would have a con-
spicuous notice of the meeting placed outside the
hall where the meeting is to take place.

I would draft, or have drafted, a motion or motions
to be submitted to the meeting ; and I should
personally approach some fit person, submit to him
a copy of the proposed motion or motions, and
request him to act as Chairman of the meeting.
I would arrange, also, for a proposer and seconder
to each motion.

On the evening of the meeting I would see that
the hall and platform are properly lighted and
provided with the number of seats necessary. I
would, also, appoint ushers whose duty is to see
that those who are to be seated on the platform and
in the body of the hall may pass into their respective
seats without confusion or discord.

Finally, I would appoint doorkeepers, and instruct
them to refuse admission to persons under the
influence of drink, or persons who, for other reasons,
are likely to be offensive to their neighbours.

18. *The meeting being assembled, what is the first
thing to be done ?*

If a Chairman has not already been appointed.

and his name advertised, the first thing to do is to move a motion and elect a Chairman.

19. *What is the order of business at a public meeting ?*

The order of business, unless otherwise ordered by the meeting, is the order in which the questions to be discussed are presented by the promoters of the meeting.

20. *Explain the procedure that should be observed at a public meeting.*

On taking the Chair, the Chairman disposes of any formal matters that require attention ; and calls on one of the promoters of the meeting or some other person appointed for the purpose, to move a motion.

A motion, having been proposed and seconded, is open to amendment and debate, and the vote thereon is ascertained by a show of hands should the Chairman's opinion given in accordance with the voices " aye " and " no " be disputed. The meeting proceeds in this manner until all the business is dealt with or the meeting adjourned.

It has become a custom to some extent to allow to speak those only who have been selected by the promoters of the meeting, and to regard as unnecessary the taking of the voices " aye " and " no."

It is, no doubt, best to omit the voices, and to take a show of hands directly the question is put to the vote ; but to refuse some of those present the right to debate a motion, and to rule out of

order all proposed amendments (as is sometimes
done), is a practice that cannot be defended.

21. *How can the Chairman at a public meeting best
deal with the following business :*

(a) *It has been moved and seconded, " That it is
inadvisable that sectarian questions should be
introduced into general politics."*

(b) *An amendment has been moved and seconded,
" That sectarian questions often directly affect
general political questions, and should not,
therefore, be wholly excluded."*

(c) *Notice has been given of a further amendment :
" That the discussion of sectarian questions at
public meetings should not be encouraged."*

The Chairman should deal first with the original
motion (meaning the motion to which the amendments
have been moved).

The case cited in *Question* 21 often occurs at a
public meeting, and the Chairman should be prepared
to deal with it when it occurs.

A careful study of the motion and amendments
will show that the amendment proposed is a true
amendment of the motion, inasmuch as it modifies
(and therefore amends) the motion to some extent ;
while the further amendment of which notice has
been given, does not in any way refer to general
politics ; but deals solely with the discussion of
sectarian questions at public meetings.

A strict ruling would accept the proposed amendment, and require the further amendment to be moved as a separate motion.

But it is not wise to introduce fine points of order at public meetings; and the Chairman will do well to accept as an amendment anything dealing with the subject then before the meeting.

The Chairman should, therefore, in the case cited in *Question* 21, when about to " put " the question, say :

" I have here a motion and an amendment, and notice has been given of a further amendment. I intend to act in accordance with Parliamentary Practice, and shall first put the original motion to the vote.

" If the original motion is lost, the amendment will become the motion ; and I shall accept the further amendment, of which notice has been given, as the amendment.   Those who are in favour of the amendment, or further amendment, will therefore vote against the motion.

" The question is : That the motion be agreed to. Those in favour of that will hold up one hand. Those against it will hold up one hand."

The position mentioned in *Question* 21 may be further complicated if a person moves to strike words out of the original motion, to insert words in it, or add words to it ; for such amendments take precedence of other amendments.

In such a case, the Chairman should deal first with those amendments, and then " put " the question :

That the motion be agreed to ; or, That the motion, as amended, be agreed to.

When the motion, or the motion as amended, is agreed to, the other amendment and the further amendment are lost ; but, if the motion, or the motion as amended, is negatived, the motion is lost ; and the Chairman deals with the other amendment, which now becomes the motion, and may be dealt with in the same manner as the original motion. The further amendment, of which notice has been given, may now be moved, and becomes the amendment.

It is not advisable, at public meetings, to " put " the question that words shall stand. A more satisfactory method is for the Chairman to say :

" You have all heard the motion read. It is proposed to strike out these words (state the words). Those in favour of that will hold up one hand. Those against it will hold up one hand."

This method will be found useful for a public meeting, but it should not be employed elsewhere. Correct Parliamentary procedure is the best method, as will be seen from subsequent questions and answers.

MEETINGS OF ORGANIZED BODIES

22. *How are organized bodies governed ?*

Organized bodies are governed by the rules of the organization.

23. *If the rules of an organization prescribe rules of order to be observed at meetings of the organization, and these rules are in conflict with those of Parliamentary Practice, how should the Chairman decide a question of order ?*

The Chairman must decide according to the rules of the organization.

24. *What is a quorum ?*

A " quorum " is the smallest number of members who shall be present at a meeting when business is being transacted.

25. *What must the Chairman do when there is not a quorum present—*

    (a) To begin a meeting ;

    (b) During a meeting ?

When a quorum is not present the Chairman must—

(a) Postpone the meeting, after waiting a reasonable time.

(b) His attention being called thereto, adjourn the meeting.

26. *In what order or sequence should the business of the meeting be considered ?*

A quorum being present, the Chairman takes the Chair ; and the order of business is usually as follows :

The minutes of the previous meeting are read and confirmed ; or, if incorrect in any resepct, they are amended, and, as amended, confirmed by the meeting and signed by the Chairman.

Formal business is then disposed of, correspondence read and dealt with, questions answered, reports received, and motions of which notice has been given are considered.

The rest of the business is taken in the order in which it is set down on the paper, and, when there is no order paper, in the order that it is presented by the Chairman.

MOTIONS

27. *What is a motion ?*

A motion may be defined as : A formal proposal made in a deliberative assembly.

28. *What are the requirements of a motion ?*

Every motion should commence with the word " That," and be of an affirmative character ; that is, it should endeavour to declare positively the will of the meeting.

29. *What is meant by " notice of motion " ?*

As a rule, no motion can be considered unless notice of it has been previously given ; but leave to move the motion may be asked by the proposer, and, if leave is granted, the motion may be moved.

30. *Do all motions require notice ?*

The rule requiring notice of motion does not apply to motions in connection with business that the members of the organization have met to consider.

31. *How is notice of motion given ?*

Notice is given by a member (at a meeting held

previous to the meeting at which he intends to move the motion), reading out the proposed motion and handing a copy, signed by himself, to the Chairman.

32. *Must every motion be moved and seconded before being debated ?*

No debate can take place on any question until a motion has been moved and seconded, and the motion has been read to the meeting and a question " stated " thereon by the Chairman. Until this has been done, only the mover and seconder of the motion have the right to speak, and their speeches should be in support of the motion.

A motion made in committee does not require to be seconded ; nor does a formal motion.

Formal motions cannot be debated.

There are a number of formal motions used in Parliament which are not required in other assemblies —such as : That the Bill be now read first time ; or motions for the postponement, the discharge, or the removal of an Order of the Day.

In Parliament, when a motion is moved : That you do leave the Chair, the Speaker " puts " the question without debate or amendment—The question is : That I do now leave the Chair ; and if the motion is agreed to, the Chairman leaves the Chair, and the House stands adjourned until the next sitting-day.

To this extent the motion has the same effect as

a motion to adjourn the House; but it has greater
consequences; for, when the motion is moved in a
Committee on a Bill, and agreed to, the Bill is killed
for the time being. It will require to be re-introduced
and put through all stages before being passed.

In other assemblies the motion: That the Chairman do now leave the Chair, if agreed to, will have
this effect—That the Chairman should at once leave
the Chair, and the meeting stand adjourned until the
next meeting-day, while the question previously
under consideration will lapse.

If it is desired that the Chairman should leave the
Chair for some special purpose, such purpose should
be clearly stated in the motion—as, for instance:
That the Chairman do now leave the Chair so that
the meeting may go into Committee.

33. *A motion having been proposed and seconded,
how does the Chairman deal with it ?*

The Chairman must "state" a question to the
meeting; and, when the debate thereon is finished,
or, if there is no debate, he must "put" the question
to the vote.

34. *Explain the difference between "stating" the
question and "putting" the question.*

The Chairman is said to "state" the question
when he states it for the information of members.
He is said to "put" the question when he proceeds
to take the vote thereon.

35. *The following motion having been moved and seconded, " state " the question :*

> *That Parliamentary Practice is part of that branch of education known as " Civics."*

And the debate thereon being finished, show how the question is " put."

The Chairman " states " the question :

(1) The question is, That Parliamentary Practice is part of that branch of education known as " Civics."

The Chairman " puts " the question :

(2) The question is, That Parliamentary Practice is part of that branch of education known as " Civics." As many as are of that opinion will say " Aye." (He waits to hear the voices.) As many as are of the contrary opinion will say " No." (He waits to hear the voices.)

36. *The question having been " put," what is the next duty of the Chairman ?*

The Chairman declares whether " the Ayes have it," or " the Noes have it."

37. *How are questions decided or determined ?*

The question is decided when the opinion of the Chairman that " the Ayes have it " or " the Noes have it " is accepted by the meeting. When the opinion of the Chairman is challenged the question

is determined according to the votes for and against
it.

38. *Can a question be reconsidered after it has once
been decided? If so, what steps are necessary to
enable this to be done?*

When time permits notice should be given of a
motion to reconsider the question; otherwise the
member should ask for leave to move a motion to
that effect. Leave must be unanimous.

When a motion has been rejected, no motion of
the same nature can be brought forward again at
the same meeting. The Parliamentary rule is that
no motion to the same effect can be brought forward
again during the same session.

39. *How are motions of a complicated nature dealt
with by the Chairman?*

The Chairman should explain to the meeting that
it is necessary to divide the motion in parts, show
the manner in which he proposes to divide it, and
declare his intention to "put" it first in parts,
and afterwards as a whole.

40. *Should verbal motions be accepted by the
Chairman?*

It is a Parliamentary rule that motions must be
in writing but, for the convenience of other assemblies,
it is sufficient that they should be written down by
the Chairman and read to the meeting.

41. *Can a motion that has been moved and seconded be withdrawn ? If so, explain the necessary procedure.*

A motion cannot be withdrawn except by leave of the meeting.

The member who has moved the motion must, therefore, ask for leave if he desires to withdraw the motion. He cannot be compelled to withdraw it.

When leave to withdraw is asked for, the Chairman says : " Is it the pleasure of the meeting that the motion (or amendment) be withdrawn ? " and, on leave being granted, he declares the motion withdrawn.

42. *Can a motion that has been withdrawn be moved again ? If so, when ?*

A motion that has been withdrawn may be moved again at the same or a subsequent meeting.

43. *If not moved when called on by the Chairman, what becomes of a motion of which notice has been given ?*

If a motion of which notice has been given is not moved when called on by the Chairman, it lapses.

44. *How often should the Chairman " state " the question to the meeting ?*

The Chairman should " state " the question as often as he may deem necessary. He also " states " the question whenever requested to do so.

45. *How often does the Chairman " put " the question to the meeting ?*

The Chairman " puts " the question once only — except when a division is called for.

AMENDMENTS

46. *What is an amendment*

An amendment may be defined as : An alteration made, or proposed to be made, in a motion.

47. *Does every amendment require to be seconded ?*

Amendments must be seconded ; but there is an exception to the rule. They are not seconded in committees

48. *An elector at a political meeting rises and says :*

> "*I move—That a hearty vote of thanks and confidence be accorded to the candidate who has addressed us this evening.*"

The motion having been seconded, another elector rises and says :

> "*I move, as an amendment—To strike out the words ' and confidence.*' "

The amendment being seconded, how should both questions be stated ?

(a) *That of the motion ;*

(b) *That of the amendment.*

Supposing the motion and amendment to be

moved at a public meeting the question may be
" stated " as follows :

(1) The question is : That the motion be agreed
     to.

(2) The motion is : That a hearty vote of thanks
     and confidence be accorded to the candidate
     who has addressed us this evening.

      An amendment has been moved to strike
     out the words " and confidence."

      Those in favour of striking out the words
     " and confidence " will hold up one hand.

As already stated, this method is advocated for
use at public meetings only.

But let us suppose that the candidate has addressed
a meeting of the members of an organized body.
In that case the Chairman should " state " the
question as follows :

(1) The question is : That a hearty vote of thanks
     and confidence be accorded to the candidate
     who has addressed us this evening.

(2) The original question was : That a hearty
     vote of thanks and confidence be accorded to
     the candidate who has addressed us this
     evening.

      Since when it has been moved, by way of
     amendment, to strike out the words " and
     confidence."

      The question now is : That the words pro-
     posed to be struck out shall stand part of
     the motion.

49. *In what way or ways may a motion be amended ?*
A motion may be amended—

   (*a*) By striking out words.

   (*b*) By inserting words.

   (*c*) By striking out certain words and substituting other words.

   (*d*) By adding words to the motion.

   (*e*) By striking out all the words after the first word, " That," and substituting other words dealing with the same subject.

50. *Can any amendment be amended ?*
Any amendment may be amended.

51. *When a number of amendments are proposed to the same motion, in what order should the Chairman deal with them ?*

When more amendments than one are proposed to a motion, the Chairman deals with the amendment, one at a time, in the order in which they affect the words of the motion, commencing at the first word of the motion.

When words have been struck out of a motion and other words are proposed to be inserted. the Chairman should deal first with the words that are first proposed to be inserted and, if that amendment is lost, he should take other words that may be proposed to be inserted in the order in which they are moved.

When figures have been struck out, the practice

is for the Chairman to accept as the first amendment
the number which is nearest to the figures struck out ;
and, if that amendment is lost, to accept the next
nearest number, and so on.

When dates are struck out, the practice is for the
Chairman to accept as the first amendment the most
distant date, then the next most distant date, and
so on.

52. *What is a prior amendment ?*

A prior amendment is an amendment which deals
with a preceding part of the motion.

Suppose an amendment has been moved (but not
yet agreed to or negatived) affecting, say, the
twenty-first word of the motion, and a member
desires to move an amendment affecting, say, the
tenth word of the motion, the member should rise
and say : " I desire to move a prior amendment."

53. *How are prior amendments dealt with by the Chairman ?*

The Chairman should ask the mover of the amendment then before the meeting if he is willing to
withdraw his amendment for the time being, in
order that a prior amendment may be moved.

On the member consenting to do so, the Chairman
says : " The amendment before the meeting is
withdrawn," and he calls on the other member to
move his prior amendment.

But should the mover of an amendment then

before the meeting refuse to withdraw his amendment in order that a prior amendment may be moved, he cannot be compelled to do so.

By courtesy, the mover of an amendment usually withdraws in favour of a prior amendment. When he refuses to do so, the member who desired to move the prior amendment waits until the question is stated, That the motion (or the motion as amended) be agreed to, and then moves, That the motion (or the motion as amended, as the case may be) be reconsidered.

54. *When part of a motion has been amended, what other parts of it can afterwards be amended ?*

An amendment cannot be made in any part of a motion that precedes a part which has already been amended ; but any subsequent part of the motion may be amended, and words can be added at the end of the motion.

55. *The following motion has been moved and seconded :*

> *That questions in the art of Chairmanship are desirable when they impress upon the mind of the student the best methods of despatching business.*

How should the Chairman proceed while the motion is being amended ?—

    (a) *By striking out words ;*

    (b) *By inserting words ;*

 (c) *By striking out certain words and substituting*
  other words ; and

 (d) *By adding words ;*

so that the motion, as amended, will read as follows :

  That questions in Chairmanship are useful and
  desirable, in so far as they impress upon the
  mind of the student the best methods of despatching
  business, and enable him to overcome promptly
  and judiciously any difficulties that may arise.

The Chairman should, in each instance, " state "
and " put " the questions as in the following illus-
tration, and declare the result of the voting—that
is to say, whether " the Ayes have it " or " the
Noes have it " :

The Chairman " states " the question :

The question is : That questions in the art of
Chairmanship are desirable when they impress upon
the mind of the student the best methods of despatching business.

A member moves, as an amendment (a) to strike
out the words " the art of " ; and the Chairman
" states " the new question :

The original question was : That questions in the
art of Chairmanship are desirable when they impress
upon the mind of the student the best methods of
despatching business.

Since when it has been moved, by way of amendment, to strike out the words " the art of,"

The question now is : That the words proposed
to be struck out shall stand part of the motion.

The debate being finished, or, if there is no debate, the Chairman " puts " the question :

The original question was : That questions in the art of Chairmanship are desirable when they impress upon the mind of the student the best methods of despatching business.

Since when it has been moved, by way of amendment, to strike out the words " the art of."

The question now is : That the words proposed to be struck out shall stand part of the motion. As many as are of that opinion will say " Aye." As many as are of the contrary opinion will say " No."

He listens to the voices : and declares : " The Noes have it," the words are struck out.

A member then moves, as an amendment (b), to insert the words " useful and " before the word " desirable."

The Chairman " states " the question :

An amendment is moved to insert the words " useful and " before the word " desirable."

The question now is : That the words proposed to be inserted shall be so inserted.

The debate being finished, or, if there is no debate, the Chairman " puts " the question :

An amendment is moved to insert the words " useful and " before the word " desirable."

The question now is : That the words proposed to be inserted be so inserted. As many as are of that opinion will say " Aye." As many as are of the contrary opinion will say " No." (He may use the shorter formula : Those in favour say " Aye." Contrary " No.") He listens to the voices ; and declares : " The Ayes have it," the words are inserted.

A member then moves, as an amendment (c), to strike out the word " when " for the purpose of substituting the words " in so far as."

The Chairman " states " the question :

It is proposed to strike out the word " when " for the purpose of inserting, in lieu thereof, the words " in so far as."

The question now is : That the word proposed to be struck out shall stand part of the motion.

The debate being finished ; or if there is no debate, the Chairman " puts " the question :

An amendment is moved to strike out the word " when " for the purpose of inserting, in lieu thereof, the words " in so far as."

The question now is : That the word proposed to be struck out shall stand part of the motion. Those in favour of that say " Aye." Contrary " No." He listens to the voices ; and declares : " The Noes have it," the word is struck out.

The Chairman then " puts " this further question (in order to complete the amendment) :

The question now is : That the words proposed to be inserted be so inserted. Those in favour say " Aye." Contrary " No." He listens to the voices ; and declares " The Ayes have it," the words are inserted.

A member then moves, as an amendment (d), to add at the end of the motion the words " and enable him to overcome, promptly and judiciously, any difficulties that may arise."

The Chairman " states " the question :

It is proposed to add, at the end of the motion, the words " and enable him to overcome, promptly and judiciously, any difficulties that may arise."

The question now is : That the words proposed to be added be so added.

The debate being finished, or, if there is no debate, the Chairman " puts " the question :

It is proposed to add, at the end of the motion, the words " and enable him to overcome, promptly and judiciously, any difficulties that may arise."

The question now is : That the words proposed to be added shall be so added. Those in favour of that will say " Aye." Contrary " No." He listens to the voices ; and declares " The Ayes have it," the words are added.

There being no further amendments, the Chairman " puts " the motion as amended :

The question is : That questions in Chairmanship are useful and desirable, in so far as they impress upon the mind of the student the best methods of despatching business, and enable him to overcome, promptly and judiciously, any difficulties that may arise. As many as are of that opinion will say " Aye." As many as are of the contrary opinion will say " No." He listens to the voices, and declares: "The Ayes have it," the motion, as amended, is agreed to.

56. *Can a motion be amended otherwise than as already shown ?*

A motion may also be amended by striking out all the words after the first word, "That," with a view to substituting other words.

57. *A motion has been moved and seconded :*

That, in the opinion of the members of this society, some improvement is necessary in the manner in which the business of its meetings is conducted,

and to this motion an amendment has been moved and seconded, as follows :

That a code of Standing Orders and Rules of Debate be drawn up by a committee to be appointed for that purpose, and that each member be supplied with a copy thereof.

Describe the proceedings of the Chairman, and so arrange—

(a) *That the motion is agreed to and the amendment negatived ; and*

(b) *That the amendment is agreed to and the motion negatived.*

A. The Chairman " states " the question :

The question is : That, in the opinion of the members of this society, some improvement is

necessary in the manner in which the business of its
meeting is conducted.

A member moves, as an amendment (*e*), to strike
out all the words after the first word " That," for
the purpose of inserting the following words :

" A code of Standing Orders and Rules of Debate
be drawn up by a committee to be appointed for
that purpose, and that each member be supplied
with a copy thereof."

The Chairman " states " the new question :

The original question was : That, in the opinion
of the members of this society, some improvement
is necessary in the manner in which the business of
its meetings is conducted.

Since when, it has been moved, by way of amendment, to strike out all the words after the first word
' That " for the purpose of inserting the following
words :

" A code of Standing Orders and Rules of Debate
be drawn up by a Committee to be appointed for
that purpose, and that each member be supplied with
a copy thereof."

The question now is : That the words proposed
to be struck out shall stand part of the motion.

The debate being finished, or if there is no debate,
the Chairman " puts " the new question :

It is proposed to strike out all the words of the
motion, except the first word " That " for the purpose
of inserting the following words :

" A code of Standing Orders and Rules of Debate

ᴄᴇ drawn up by a Committee to be appointed for that purpose, and that each member be supplied with a copy thereof."

The question now is : That the words proposed to be struck out shall stand part of the motion. As many as are of that opinion will say " Aye." As many as are of the contrary opinion will say " No." He listens to the voices ; and declares, " the Ayes have it," the words stand.

The meeting having decided that the words shall stand, the amendment is lost, and certain words of the motion have been agreed to. These words cannot now be altered or amended, unless the motion is reconsidered as a whole ; but words may be added at the end of the motion.

There being no amendment to add words to the motion, the Chairman now " puts " the motion as a whole ; for so far only part of the motion has been agreed to. The word " That " has not yet been agreed to ; and the Chairman, therefore, " puts " the motion as a whole :

The question is : That, in the opinion of the members of this society, some improvement is necessary in the manner in which the business of its meeting is conducted. As many as are of that opinion will say " Aye." As many as are of the contrary opinion will say " No." He listens to the voices ; and declares, " the Ayes have it,' the motion is agreed to.

This disposes of the first part of *Question* 57.

B. The Chairman " states " the question of the original motion. The amendment is moved, and the Chairman " states " the new question. The debate being finished ; or, if there is no debate, the Chairman " puts " the new question :

The original question was : That, in the opinion of the members of this society, some improvement is necessary in the manner in which business of its meetings is conducted. Since, when, it has been moved, by way of amendment, to strike out all the words after the first word " That " for the purpose of inserting the following words :

" A code of Standing Orders and Rules of Debate be drawn up by a Committee to be appointed for that purpose, and that each member be supplied with a copy thereof."

The question now is : That the words proposed to be struck out shall stand part of the motion. He listens to the voices ; and declares, " the Noes have it," the words are struck out.

The Chairman then " puts " the amendment :

The question is : That the words proposed to be inserted be so inserted. As many as are of that opinion will say " Aye." As many as are of the contrary opinion will say " No." He listens to the voices ; and declares, " the Ayes have it," the words are inserted.

The Chairman now " puts " the amendment as a whole :

The question is : That a code of Standing Orders

and Rules of Debate be drawn up by a Committee to be appointed for that purpose, and that each member be supplied with a copy thereof. As many as are of that opinion will say " Aye." As many as are of the contrary opinion will say " No." He listens to the voices ; and declares, " the Ayes have it," the amendment is agreed to.

This disposes of the second part of *Question* 57.

It is necessary to remember that any proposed amendment may be amended, and that, therefore, words proposed to be inserted may be amended. The words must, however, be amended before they are inserted in the place of words struck out.

Words proposed to be inserted may be amended in the same manner as a motion—that is to say, (a) By striking out words, (b) by inserting words, (c) by striking out certain words and substituting other words, (d) by adding words, or all the words proposed to be inserted may be negatived, and other words agreed to and inserted.

When words proposed to be inserted are amended, the Chairman " puts " the question :

That the words proposed to be inserted as amended be so inserted ; and, this question being agreed to, he " puts " the whole of the amendment, as amended.

58. *How should the Chairman proceed if he desires to test the feeling of the meeting in regard to the motion*

and the amendment (that is to say, to ascertain whether the meeting prefers to consider the motion or the amendment)? Give an example from the motion and amendment in the preceding question.

If the Chairman desires to test the feeling of the meeting as to the motion and amendment, he should take the first few words of the motion, and " put " the question.

It is proposed to strike out these words (read the words) for the purpose of inserting other words. The question is : That the words proposed to be struck out shall stand part of the motion. He should act according to the decision of the meeting.

Let us suppose that the motion and amendment dealt with in *Question* 57 are before a meeting, and the Chairman desires to test the feeling of members as to the motion and amendment.

In such a case the Chairman can take as a test, the words of the motion, " That in the opinion of," and explain to the meeting that if these words stand, he will deal with the remainder of the motion, and the amendment will be lost ; but that if the words are struck out, the motion will be lost, and he will deal with the amendment.

The Chairman therefore " puts " the question :

It is proposed to strike out these words : " That in the opinion of," for the purpose of inserting the words of the amendment.

The question now is : That the words proposed to be struck out shall stand part of the motion.

If the Chairman finds that " the Ayes have it,"
he declares the amendment lost, and then deals with
the remaining words of the motion.   If the remaining
words of the motion are not amended he " puts '
the question : That the motion be agreed to ; but
should the remaining words of the motion be amended
he " puts " the question : That the motion, as
amended, be agreed to.

Should the Chairman find, when he " puts " the
question (That the words proposed to be struck out
shall stand part of the motion), that " the Noes have
it," he declares the motion lost and proceeds to deal
with the amendment, which now takes the place of
the original motion.

59. *What is the position when both the motion and
the amendment have been negatived ?*

When both the motion and the amendment are
negatived, there is nothing before the meeting, and
another motion may be moved.

60. *What is meant by " a direct negative " ?*

By " a direct negative " is meant the insertion of
the word " not " in a motion, so that it will contradict
the original intention of the motion.

61. *Should the Chairman accept an amendment
which is a direct negative ?*

The Chairman should not accept an amendment

which is a direct negative of the motion when the object of the proposed amendment may be attained by voting against the motion. He should accept the proposed amendment when its intention is to emphasize the will of the meeting.

DIVISIONS

62. *What is a division ?*

A member who does not agree to the opinion of the Chairman that " the Ayes have it " or " the Noes have it," may call for a division.

In Parliament, where division lobbies are provided, the Speaker, when his opinion is challenged, orders : " the Ayes will go to the right," " the Noes to the left." Members then pass into the lobbies marked " Aye " and " No," according to how they wish their votes to be recorded, and their names are recorded as voting for or against the question. This method of voting is called " a division."

The opinion of the Speaker that " the Ayes have it " or " the Noes have it " is challenged in this manner : When the Speaker declares " the Ayes have it," a member who has given his vote with the " Noes " calls out " the Noes have it " : or when the Speaker declares " the Noes have it," a member who has given his voice with the " Ayes " calls out " the Ayes have it " ; and the Speaker then divides the House on the question.

It is a Parliamentary rule that a member who has given his voice with the " Ayes " must vote " Aye "

when the division is taken ; and a member who has
given his voice with the " Noes " must vote " No."

63. *What is the best method of taking a division—*
    (a) *At a public meeting ?*
    (b) *In small meetings—such as those of a local
    body or a committee of management ?*
    (c) *In general meetings of members of an organiza-
    tion ?*
*State also in regard to (c) the necessary steps to be
taken by the Chairman when a division is called for.*

(1) The best method of taking a division is—

(a) At a public meeting ; to call for a show of
hands.

(b) At small meetings—such as those of a local
governing body or a committee of management, to call the roll of the members present,
and to require each member to give his voice
" Aye " or " No."

(c) At general meetings of members of an organized
body, or at conferences where a large number
of delegates are present, to require those
voting " Aye " to stand up, and then to
remain standing until they are counted. Then
to require those voting " No " to do likewise.

(2) When the Chairman's opinion that " the Ayes
have it " or " the Noes have it " is challenged, the
Chairman " puts " the question again. If the Chairman's opinion is again challenged, he appoints two
' tellers " (one of whom should be chosen from

among those intending to vote " Aye " and the other from among those intending to vote " No "), whose duty shall be to count the voters " Aye " and " No."

The Chairman then explains the manner in which he intends to take the division, and calls on members to vote.

When a division has been taken the " tellers " report to the Chairman and the Chairman announces to the meeting the number of members who have voted " Aye," and the number who have voted " No," and declares, according to the majority, " the Ayes have it," or " the Noes have it."

In Parliament, four " tellers " are appointed (two for the " Ayes " and two for the " Noes "), but two " tellers " will be found sufficient for other assemblies. No " tellers " are required when the roll is called and members give their voices " Aye " and " No."

64. *The numbers of those voting in a division (for and against the motion or amendment) being equal, how is the question determined ?*

When the numbers of those voting " Aye " and " No " are equal, the Chairman gives a casting-vote, and decides according to the majority.

DEBATE

65. *What is a debate?*

A " Debate " may be defined as—a discussion that takes place upon a question submitted for consideration to a deliberative assembly.

66. *What is meant by the expression: " to debate a question " ?*

A member may be said " to debate a question " when he addresses himself to the Chair in order to discuss a question submitted for consideration to a meeting.

67. *Can every motion that is moved and seconded be debated?*

As a rule, any motion that is moved and seconded may be debated, but there are exceptions to this rule. Formal motions—such as, That the Chairman do now leave the Chair, cannot be debated.

68. *Can the motion: " That the meeting do now adjourn " be debated?*

The answer is : That the motion—" That the meeting do now adjourn "—may be debated in certain cases.

When it is moved with the object of superseding a question a debate may take place, and the debate may be upon either the question then under discussion or the question of adjournment. The Chairman, however, has discretionary power when the motion to adjourn is moved in order to conclude a meeting. If he allows debate he must confine the debate strictly to the question of adjournment ; but if he is of opinion that the motion to adjourn is moved for the purpose of obstruction or in abuse of the rules of debate, he may refuse to allow any debate and " put " the question forthwith. He does not, as a rule, allow debate unless a time or place is stated in the motion or moved by way of amendment.

The motion to adjourn the House is used in Parliament in different ways—

(1) To discuss answers given by ministers to questions.

(2) To supersede a question under discussion.

(3) To fix a time or place different to the usual time or meeting-place.

(4) To conclude a sitting.

When moved to discuss answers to questions the motion, That the House do now adjourn, is subject to certain conditions specified in the Standing Orders.

When moved to supersede a question, it is sometimes used for the purpose of " Stonewalling."

When moved to fix a time or place other than the usual time and meeting-place, it is moved in this form : That the House *at its rising* do adjourn till

—— at —— And the motion may be moved at any convenient time during the sitting.

When moved to conclude a sitting it is moved in this form : That the House do now adjourn.

69. *May every amendment be debated ?*
Every amendment may be debated.

70. *Can any debate be adjourned ?*
Any debate may be adjourned.

71. *May a motion to adjourn the debate be debated ?*
A motion to adjourn the debate may be debated ; but members must confine their speeches to giving reasons for or against the adjournment of the debate. They may not speak on the main question in debate.

72. *Can a member who has spoken to a question before the meeting move the adjournment of the debate thereon ?*
A member who has spoken to a question before the meeting cannot move the adjournment of the debate.

The rule in Parliament is, that, if a member moves the adjournment of the debate and the motion for adjournment is negatived, the member loses his right to speak in the debate, but, if the motion to adjourn the debate is agreed to, the member who has moved the adjournment of the debate has the right to be first heard when the debate is resumed.

73. *What is an " interrupted " debate ?*

A debate is said to be " interrupted " when it is stopped for a short period for any good reason— such as, to enable the Chairman to make necessary announcements ; or, in order that the meeting may consider a matter that is urgent.

74. *How may a debate be interrupted ?*

A debate may also be interrupted by a question of order, by want of a quorum, or by adjournment of the meeting.

> The practice is that a member who raises a point of order shall be allowed to explain it before the Chairman gives his ruling ; for the ruling of the Chairman, when given, is final for the time being.

When the point of order has been disposed of, the debate is resumed at the point where it was interrupted.

75. *What must a member do when he is " called to order " by the Chairman ?*

A member " called to order " by the Chairman must sit down.

76. *When a member has been " called to order " by the Chairman, and has resumed his seat, has he the right to finish his speech ?*

A member " called to order " by the Chairman,

and who has resumed his seat, loses the right to
finish his speech.

> The Chairman, as a rule, only " calls to order "
> a member who persists in ignoring a ruling
> from the Chair, after having been warned by
> the Chairman. Being "called to order " is,
> in reality, a penalty for contumacy.

The Chairman usually says to a member : " I
must ask you to confine your remarks to the question
under discussion," or " It seems to me that you are
going beyond the scope of the question we are
discussing " ; or " I have already warned you that
you must confine your remarks to the question
before the meeting. If you offend again, I shall
call you to order."

77. Can a member challenge the ruling of the Chairman ? If so, in what manner ?

Any ruling of the Chairman may be objected to,
and a motion moved, That the ruling of the Chairman
(state the ruling) be disagreed to ; and, when time
permits, notice should be given of the motion.

> When a motion objecting to the ruling of the
> Chairman has been moved and seconded, the
> Chairman " states " the question, The ques-
> tion is, That my ruling (reads the ruling
> objected to) be disagreed to.

The Chairman then explains to the meeting his
reasons for so ruling, and cites the authorities (if
any) on which he bases his ruling. The motion

may now be debated; and, when the debate is finished, or, if there is no debate, the Chairman "puts" the question, and "rules" in accordance with the decision of the meeting (whether that decision be correct or otherwise).

In some organized bodies, it is provided in the rules that a certain number of members shall stand up in their places, in order to support an objection to the ruling of the Chairman, before a motion for that purpose may be accepted by the Chairman, a practice that has much to recommend it. In Parliament any member may challenge the ruling of the Speaker.

Some Chairmen like to explain their rulings, and take every opportunity to do so. This is, usually, an indication of a weak Chairman, who, sooner or later, will land himself in a difficult position. A Chairman should never give reasons for his rulings, unless a ruling is challenged.

78. *What is a "superseded" debate?*

A debate is said to be "superseded" when the question then under debate is set aside or other business takes its place.

79. *In what manner may a debate be superseded?*

A debate may be superseded—

(a) By a motion: That the meeting do now adjourn.

(b) By a member calling attention to the fact that a quorum is not present.

(c) By a motion being agreed to : That the meeting proceed to consider the next business.

(d) By " the Previous Question."

80. *Explain what is meant by " the Previous Question."*

" The Previous Question " is a motion that enables a meeting to set aside a question in regard to which it does not wish to express an opinion. It is used when the mover of a motion will not ask leave to withdraw a motion that the meeting desires should be withdrawn.

81. *Who may move " the Previous Question " ?*

Any member who has not yet spoken to the question then before the meeting may rise in his place and say, " I move ' the Previous Question,' " and proceed to debate the original motion in the same manner as if he had not moved " the Previous Question."

When the member has resumed his seat, the Chairman says, " ' The Previous Question ' has been moved," and asks, " Is the motion seconded ? "

If the motion is not seconded, it lapses ; but, on its being seconded, the Chairman " states " the question in this form—which is the form used in the House of Commons—The question is : That *that* question be not now put.

82. *A motion has been moved and seconded—*

> *That all education, from the primary school to the University, both included, should be free,*

and *" the Previous Question "* *has been moved by another member.*

" State " and " put " the necessary questions, and so arrange that the original motion is agreed to.

The Chairman " states " the question: " The original question was

> That all education, from the primary school to the University, both included, should be free."

Since when, " the Previous Question " has been moved. Is that seconded ?

" The Previous Question " being seconded, the Chairman " states " the new question—The question is : That *that* question (meaning the question of the original motion) be not now put.

The debate being finished, or, if there is no debate, the Chairman " puts " the question :

The question is : That that question be not now put.

As many as are of that opinion will say " Aye." As many as are of the contrary opinion will say " No." He listens to the voices, and declares " The Noes have it," " the Previous Question " is negatived.

The meeting, having voted against " the Previous Question," has decided that the original motion *shall* be now put. The Chairman, therefore, " puts " the question, without further amendment or debate,

"That all education, from the primary school
to the University, both included, should be
free."

He listens to the voices, and declares : "The Ayes
have it, the motion is agreed to."

83. *Does " the Previous Question " prevent further
debate on the original motion ?*

The motion of " the Previous Question " does not
in any way affect the debate on the original motion.
The debate continues as if " the Previous Question "
had not been moved.

84. *What does the Chairman do when " the Previous
Question " is agreed to ?*

When " the Previous Question " is agreed to, the
Chairman declares : " The Ayes have it, the motion
lapses."

85. *How does the Chairman deal with the original
motion when " the Previous Question " is negatived ?*

When " the Previous Question " is negatived, the
Chairman " puts " the original motion without
further amendment or debate.

86. *Can " the Previous Question " be moved when
an amendment is before the meeting ?*

" The Previous Question " cannot be " put "
when an amendment is before the meeting. The
amendment must first be disposed of.

87. *Can " the Previous Question " be amended ?*
" The Previous Question " cannot be amended.

88. *Can " the Previous Question " be superseded ?*
" The Previous Question " may be superseded by a motion to adjourn the meeting.

89. *Can the debate on " the Previous Question " be adjourned ?*
The debate on " the Previous Question " can be adjourned.

90. *If the debate on " the Previous Question " is adjourned, can the debate on the original motion be continued ? If not, why not ?*
The debate on the original motion cannot be resumed if the debate on " the Previous Question " is adjourned ; for the reason that it is the same debate.

91. *What is the sole object of " the Previous Question " ?*
The sole object of " the Previous Question " is to withdraw a motion (after it has been debated) which the mover refuses to withdraw. Its object is attained when " the Ayes have it."

92. *Is the original motion finally disposed of when " the Previous Question " is agreed to ?*
The original motion is not finally disposed of

when " the Previous Question " is agreed to. It
lapses, and may be moved again by leave of the
meeting, or when notice of motion has been again
given.

93. *What is a " lapsed " motion ?*
A motion is said to have " lapsed "—
   (a) If not moved when called on by the Chairman.
   (b) If less than a quorum vote in a division on
       the motion.
   (c) If " the Previous Question " is agreed to.

94. *Can a motion that has lapsed, or one that has
by leave been withdrawn, be moved again ?*
A motion that has lapsed may be re-introduced,
and a motion that has by leave been withdrawn may
be moved again at the same or a subsequent meeting.

LIMITATION OF DEBATE

95. *What is a time-limit ?*

A time-limit is a personal closure. It limits the time a member may speak to a question.

96. *What is the object of a time-limit and the closure ?*

The object of a time-limit is to prevent unnecessary debate. The closure is used, principally, to put an end to organized obstruction on the part of the minority.

97. *When the rules of an organization do not prescribe a time-limit to speeches, what must be done before one can be enforced ?*

When the rules of an organized body do not provide a time-limit, a resolution of the meeting is necessary before one can be enforced, and its restrictions must be stated in the resolution.

98. *In what respect does the closure differ from a time-limit ?*

The closure differs from the time-limit in so far as (if agreed to) it stops all debate, while the time limit merely limits the time allowed to a member in which to debate a question.

99. *What is the ordinary form of the closure ?*

The ordinary form of closure is : That the question be now put.

> A member may at any stage of a debate move : That the question be now put ; and, if seconded, the motion for the closure shall be " put " to the meeting so soon as the member then speaking has finished his speech.

100. *The ordinary form of closure having been moved and seconded, " state " the question.*

The ordinary form of closure having been proposed and seconded, the Chairman " states " the question.

The question is : That the question be now put.

101. *The closure having been " put," what does the Chairman do when " the Ayes have it " ?*

When the motion for the closure is agreed to, the Chairman " puts " the question under debate without further discussion.

102. *What becomes of the original motion when the closure has been " put " and " the Noes have it " ?*

When the motion for the closure is negatived, the debate on the motion is resumed at the point where it was interrupted.

BREACHES OF ORDER

103. *How is order enforced at a public meeting ?*

To enforce order at a public meeting, the Chairman (if necessary) calls on the police to assist him, and the offender is ejected from the meeting.

104. *What is necessary in order that breaches of order may be dealt with effectively by the Chairman of an organized body ?*

Provision for the enforcement by order should be made in the rules of every organized body.

It should be provided in the rules that a member declared by the Chairman to be guilty of disorderly conduct shall, on motion made and agreed to, be punished—

    (*a*) By being evicted from the meeting ;

    (*b*) By being suspended for a fixed period from attendance at meetings ; or until he offers a satisfactory apology ; or

    (*c*) By being fined ;

and " disorderly conduct " may be defined as—

    (*a*) Refusing to vote ;

    (*b*) Using objectionable words, and refusing

to withdraw them or offer a satisfactory
apology ;

(c) Wilfully disturbing the orderly conduct of
business ; and

(d) Disobeying an order from the Chair.

The Standing Orders and Rules of Debate given
in *How to Conduct a Meeting* provide all that is
necessary for the conduct of business, including the
enforcement of order ; but, before they can be
applied, a resolution to that effect must be adopted
at a general meeting.

105. *In what way can the Chairman enforce obedience
to the Chair when there is no provision in the rules
relating to breaches of order ?*

When there is no provision in the rules of an
organized body for the enforcement of order, and
rules of order have not been adopted, the Chairman
should act in accordance with his knowledge of
Parliamentary Practice or according to custom
(which, in fact, is also based on Parliamentary
Practice).

But it is of the utmost importance that the proceedings at meetings should be conducted in a
proper manner ; otherwise it may be found, when a
matter is investigated in a court of law, that the
proceedings were illegal. In such a case, money
may have been voted and paid away illegally ; and
the executive officers of the organization will be held
personally liable for the amount so voted.

106. *What is meant by the expression " serious disorder " ; and how should it be dealt with ?*

Serious disorder means disorder that involves a breach of the peace ; and breaches of the peace may be dealt with in accordance with the provisions of the law.

COMMITTEES

107. *What is meant by "a Committee of the whole"?*

Any meeting may, on motion agreed to, resolve itself into a Committee of the whole.

108. *How is a Committee of the whole set up?*

A Committee of the whole is set up by a motion agreed to, that this meeting do now resolve itself into a Committee of the whole.

109. *What rules of procedure are observed in a Committee of the whole?*

The rules of procedure used in an ordinary meeting are the rules which govern all committees, except the rule limiting the number of times a member may speak and the rule requiring a motion or an amendment to be seconded.

110. *What is the principal object of going into Committee of the whole?*

The principal object in going into Committee of the whole is to enable the members to discuss more freely the matter referred to them and its details.

111. *Does the Chairman of an organized body leave the Chair when the meeting resolves itself into a Committee of the whole ?*

The Chairman of the meeting does not leave the Chair when the meeting goes into Committee of the whole. He conducts the business as in open meeting.

112. *In what respect can the Committee of the whole be often usefully employed ?*

The Committee of the whole can often be usefully employed ; and, especially, when drafts containing a large number of paragraphs have to be considered. The paragraphs can then be taken *seriatim*, and reconsidered as often as desired before being agreed to or negatived as a whole.

113. *Are speeches reported that are made in Committee of the whole ?*

The speeches made in any Committee are not reported.

114. *A motion having been moved and seconded to go into Committee, " state " the question thereon.*

A motion having been proposed and seconded, That this meeting do now resolve itself into a Committee of the whole, the Chairman " states " the question : The question is : That I do now leave the Chair in order that the meeting may go into Committee of the whole for the purpose of (state the purpose).

115. *Has the Chairman of a Committee of the whole a deliberative as well as a casting-vote ?*

The Chairman of a Committee of the whole has a casting-vote only.

116. *What is a Select Committee ?*

A Select Committee is a Committee set up to consider and report upon a matter specially referred to it.

117. *What is a Standing Committee ?*

A Standing Committee is a Select Committee set up for a fixed period. Its duty is to consider and report on matters specially referred to it.

In Parliament, such Committees are set up at the commencement of each session, and report, from time to time, to the House. They are termed " Sessional Committees." Municipal Councils have similar Committees, such as a Finance Committee, while many organized bodies have Committees of Management.

118. *Are the same rules of order observed in a Standing Committee as in a Select Committee ?*

The same rules of order and procedure are observed in all Committees.

119. *How is a Select Committee set up ?*

A Select Committee is set up by resolution of a meeting.

120. *Of how many members may a Select Committee consist ?*

A Select Committee usually consists of not less than three or more than nine members—one of whom is the member who has moved the motion to set up the Committee.

If it is desired to have a larger Committee, the Standing Order may be suspended, on motion agreed to, to enable this to be done.

121. *May a Select Committee be elected by ballot ? If so, what steps are necessary ?*

A Select Committee may be elected by ballot. If three members rise in their places and demand a ballot, the Committee must be elected by ballot, and, when there is an equality of votes in the ballot, the Chairman decides by lot who shall be the member of the Committee.

122. *How many members are necessary to form a quorum of a Select Committee ?*

In all Select Committees three members form a quorum

123. *Who calls the first meeting of a Select Committee ?*

The first meeting of a Select Committee is called by the Official Chairman at the request of the member who moved for the appointment of the Committee.

124. *Who shall be Chairman of a Select Committee ?*

The mover of a Select Committee is usually appointed the Chairman of the Committee ; but the members of the Committee may decide otherwise. When the Official Chairman of the organized body is a member of the Committee he has the right to preside, if he cares to do so.

125. *Have the Chairman of a Select Committee and the Chairman of a Standing Committee a deliberative as well as a casting-vote ?*

The Chairman of a Select Committee and the Chairman of a Standing Committee have a deliberative as well as a casting-vote.

In such Committees, the Chairman takes part in the discussions that arise, and even proposes motions for the consideration of the Committee. In fact, he combines the duty of a member with that of a Chairman.

126. *Who maintains order in Committee ?*

Order is maintained in any Committee by the Chairman.

127. *What rules of procedure are observed in a Select or a Standing Committee ?*

The rules of procedure are the same in a Select or Standing Committee as in a Committee of the whole.

128. *How is disorder in Committees dealt with ?*

Breaches of order that occur in any Committee are reported to and dealt with by the members of the organization in open meeting.

129. *When is the duty of a Select Committee ended ?*

The duty of a Select Committee is fulfilled when its Chairman brings up his report to a meeting of the organization.

130. *How are reports of Committees dealt with ?*

The reports of all Committees are dealt with by the members of the organization in open meeting assembled.

MISCELLANEOUS QUESTIONS

131. *What are the minutes of a meeting ?*

The minutes of a meeting are an official record of the business transacted at that meeting.

132. *Should reference be made in the minutes to speeches delivered at the meeting ?*

No reference to speeches, or reports thereof, should appear in the minutes.

133. *What should be set forth in the minutes ?*

The minutes should be short and concise, and show the place, date, and hour of the meeting, who presided, the number of members present, the business transacted, and the hour of adjournment.

It is advisable that the names of the mover and seconder of motions and amendments should be recorded in the minutes.

134. *What is meant by " The minutes of the previous meeting were read and confirmed " ?*

The business of a meeting is commenced by the Secretary or Clerk reading, at the request of the Chairman, the minutes of the previous meeting; or, in the case of a first meeting, by reading a statement showing the authority by which the meeting is convened.

When the minutes are read the Chairman puts the question, without a motion having been moved. The question is: That I do confirm these minutes as read; or, he may ask, " Is it your pleasure that I do confirm these minutes ? "

The only question that can arise from the reading of the minutes is: Are they correct, or are they incorrect ? If correct, they must be confirmed by the meeting. If incorrect, they are at once corrected, the corrections initialled by the Chairman, and confirmed as amended.

When the meeting has agreed that the minutes shall be confirmed, or confirmed as amended, they are immediately signed by the Chairman as having been so confirmed.

135. *It sometimes happens, as in the case of maritime organizations, that none of the members who were present when the business was transacted is present when the minutes are read for confirmation. What should be done, therefore, to certify their accuracy ?*

The Chairman who presided should sign the minutes as correct. Minutes which have not yet

been confirmed are accepted as evidence in a court
of law when signed by the presiding Chairman.

When a meeting is a final one—such as the last
meeting of a Committee—a motion should be agreed
to, before adjourning, authorizing the Chairman to
confirm the minutes.

136. *Explain the expression, " Business arising out
of the minutes of the previous meeting was then dealt
with."*

The expression means that business unfinished at
the previous meeting, or business consequent on that
done at the previous meeting, was further considered
or finally dealt with. Such business usually takes
precedence of any new business.

137. *How is correspondence brought before a meeting ?*

The letters are read to the meeting by the Clerk
or Secretary, and are afterwards considered in the
order in which they have been read.

A practice has grown up in which, after the
whole of the correspondence has been read, a
motion is required, that the correspondence be
received.

It would be more in accordance with Parliamentary
Practice, when the meeting does not wish to consider
a letter, to move : That the letter lie upon the
table. The effect of this resolution (for a motion
agreed to becomes a resolution of the meeting)

would be that no further notice would be taken of the
letter unless a particular motion were moved in
regard to it.

138. *How should correspondence of a libellous or
grossly offensive character be treated ?*
The Chairman should suppress such correspondence.

139. *What questions may be asked at a meeting ?*
Any question referring to the business of the
meeting or concerning the affairs of the organization.

140. *Who may ask and who may be asked a
question ?*
Any member may ask a question addressed to the
Chairman or to any member able to answer with
authority.

141. *When should reports be brought up ?*
Reports are generally received at any convenient
time during a meeting ; but, if ready, should be
presented when called for by the Chairman after
" Questions."

142. *What is the further procedure when a report is
presented ?*
The member presenting a report (usually the
Chairman of the Committee that drew up the report)
moves : That the report be read ; and when this

is done, moves another motion : That the report be adopted ; or he may explain the report and move · That the report do lie upon the table.

143. *What is the effect of a motion agreed to, That the report do lie upon the table ?*

The report is then available for the information and use of members, and, if the Press be admitted to the meeting, it is also available for the information of reporters. Nothing further is done in connection with the report unless a particular motion in regard to it is moved and agreed to.

144. *What are the Orders of the Day ?*

Any business set down by a previous meeting for consideration on a certain day, or any business which must, in accordance with the rules of the organization, be considered on that day, is an Order of the Day.

145. *A meeting having resolved to donate a sum of money for a certain purpose, can the same meeting at a later stage of the proceedings rescind the resolution, or can a subsequent meeting do so ?*

As notice of motion is necessary ; the resolution cannot be rescinded at the same meeting. It may be rescinded at a subsequent meeting, but notice of motion must have been given previous to the holding of the subsequent meeting.

146. *If notice of motion is given to rescind a resolution, what is the duty of the Executive Officers as regards the resolution proposed to be rescinded ?*

It is their duty to withhold action until an opportunity has been given to consider the motion to rescind.

SPECIAL MEETINGS

147. *What is a special meeting?*

In the rules of an organization there is, or should be, provision for the holding of special meetings to confirm important resolutions, or for the consideration of matters affecting the constitution of the organization.

148. *How are special meetings convened?*

Special meetings are convened by notice posted to members or by newspaper advertisement.

149. *What should be stated in the notice or advertisement which calls a special meeting?*

The time and place of meeting and the business to be considered thereat should be stated.

150. *Should the words " and general " be included in the notice?*

The words " and general " should not be included in the notice, for the reason that only the business stated in the notice can be considered at a special meeting. The introduction of additional business would destroy the "special" character of the meeting.

151. *Can a general meeting and a special meeting be held on the same day ?*

The two meetings may be held on the same day, but there should be an interval, however short, between the meetings. Suppose that the special meeting precedes the general meeting, the Chairman should, at the conclusion of the special meeting, declare the meeting closed and leave the Chair. He can then resume the Chair and the general meeting be held. The same precaution should be observed when the general meeting precedes the special meeting. In such a case, it is of importance that the time of commencement and conclusion of the business of each meeting should be clearly stated in the minutes.

COMPANY MEETINGS

152. *In what respect does a company meeting principally differ from other meetings?*

The principal difference is that meetings of the shareholders of a company deal with rights of property, and are governed by law and by the Articles of Association.

153. *Are the ordinary rules of order observed in a meeting of shareholders?*

The ordinary rules of order are observed, but they should be more strictly applied, as time is of greater value and the responsibility of the Directors greater.

154. *Why is the responsibility of the Directors greater than that of (say) the Executive Officers of a trade union organization?*

The responsibility of the Directors is greater on account of the legal character of the proceedings and the greater personal liability of the Directors.

155. *What general meetings are held by Companies ?*

General meetings—at which any shareholder is entitled to be present—are of two kinds : Ordinary and Extraordinary.

156. *What is an Ordinary General Meeting ?*

An Ordinary General Meeting is a meeting ordered to be held by the Articles of Association.

157. *What is an Extraordinary General Meeting ?*

An Extraordinary General Meeting is one that arises out of an Ordinary General Meeting.

158. *How are Extraordinary General Meetings convened ?*

Extraordinary General Meetings are convened by the Directors or by requisition of the shareholders.

159. *Who presides at a Company Meeting ?*

The Chairman of the Board of Directors usually presides, as provided by the Articles of Association. When no Director is present—or, if present, unwilling to act—the shareholders may elect a Chairman.

160. *Are the qualifications of the Chairman of a Company Meeting different from those of another Chairman ?*

The Chairman of a Company Meeting should, in addition to the ordinary qualifications of a Chairman,

possess a knowledge of Company law regarding the
duties of the Chairman of a Company Meeting.
When decisions involving points of law are to be
given he should consult the legal adviser of the
company, who should be present at the meeting.

161. *What should the Chairman do if a quorum is
not present to commence the meeting ?*
He should wait an hour before declaring the meeting
adjourned.

162. *What business may be considered at a Company
Meeting ?*
Only the business set forth in the notice calling
the meeting can be considered.

163. *What is meant by " voting by proxy " ?*
Where proxies are allowed, a shareholder unable
to be present at the meeting may appoint an agent
to exercise his vote or votes. " To vote by proxy "
means to vote by the agency of another.

164. *What is an Extraordinary Resolution ?*
An Extraordinary Resolution is a motion, of
which notice has been given, passed by not less than
three-fourths of the shareholders present, or voting
by proxy, at a General Meeting.

165. *What is a Special Resolution ?*
A Special Resolution is a motion, of which notice

has been given, passed by a majority of not less than three-fourths of the shareholders present, or voting by proxy, at a General Meeting; and confirmed by a bare majority at a subsequent General Meeting of which notice has been given.

INDEX

The references are to paragraph numbers.

Adjournment—
  of debate, 70–2
  of meeting, 68
Amendments, 46–61
  All may be debated, **69**
  Amendment of, **50**
  At public meeting, 21
  Defined, **46**
  Different, **49**
  Illustrated, **55, 57**
  Negatived, **59**
  Order of reception, **51**
  Other words substituted, 56
  Prior, **52, 53**
  Ruled out, **8**
  Seconded, **47**
  Words added, **54**

Breaches of order, 103–6

Casting-vote, 4, 64, 115, 125
Chairman, 1–15
  Casting-vote of, 4, 64, 115, 125
  Deliberative vote of, 125
  Duties of, 4, 10–13
  Power to adjourn, **15**
  Principal qualifications, 1, 160
  Proceedings of, illustrated, **55, 57**

Prompt decision, **2**
Ruling challenged, **77**
Tests meeting, **58**
To leave the chair, **32**
Vote of, **14**
Closure, 96, 98–102
Committees, 107–30
  Of the whole, 107–**15**
  Procedure in, 118
  Select, 116, 130
  Standing, 117
Company Meetings, 152–65
  Business considered at, 162
  Chairman's qualifications, 160
  Extraordinary General Meetings, 157, 158
  Extraordinary Resolution, 164
  General meetings of, 155
  Nature of, 152
  Ordinary General Meetings, 156
  Quorum not present, 161
  Responsibility of directors, 153, 154
  Rules of order, 153
  Special Resolution, 165
  Voting by proxy, 163
  Who presides at, 159

Correspondence, 137
  Grossly offensive, 138
  Libellous, 138

Debate, 65–94
  Adjournment of, 70–2
  Closure of, 96, 98–102
  Defined, 65, 66
  Interrupted, 73, 74
  Superseded, 78, 79
  Time-limit, 95–8
Direct negative, 60, 61
Directors, 153, 154, 159
Disorder, serious, 106
Divisions, 62, 64
  Defined, 62
  Methods of taking, 63

Extraordinary Resolution, 164

Formal motions, 32, 67
Formal questions, 4

Interrupted debate, 73, 74

Leave to withdraw, 41
Limitation of debate, 95–102

Meetings—
  Adjournment of, 68
  Correspondence read at, 137, 138
  Minutes of, 131–6
  Of companies, 152–65
  Special, 147–51
Members—
  Called to order, 75, 76
  May speak, 67, 69, 81
Minutes of meeting, 131–6
Miscellaneous Questions, 131–46
  Correspondence, 137, 138
  Minutes, 131–6
  Orders of the Day, 144

Questions asked, 139, 140
Reports, 141–3
Resolution rescinded, 145, 146
Motions, 27–45
  At public meeting, 21
  Complicated, 39
  Defined, 28
  Direct negative, 60, 61
  Formal, 32, 67
  How amended, 49
  Illustrated, 55, 57
  Lapsed, 43, 93, 94
  Moved and seconded, 32
  Negatived, 59
  Notice of, 29–31, 38
  Other words substituted, 56
  Rejected, 38
  Ruled out, 8
  Verbal, 40
  Withdrawn, 41, 42

Notice of motion, 29–31, 38

Offensive expressions, 4–7
Order—
  Breaches of, 103–6
  Maintained, 4
  Member called to, 75, 76
  Point of, 74
Orders of the Day, 144
Organized Bodies, 22–6
  How governed, 22
  Order of business, 26
  Quorum, 24, 25
  Rules of order, 23

Proxies, 163
Public meetings, 16–21
  Amendments at, 21
  Appointment of Chairman, 18
  Motions at, 21

Order of business at, 19
Procedure at, 20
To convene, 17
Point of order, 74
Previous Question, 80–92

Question—
How decided, 37
Illustrated, 55, 57
Previous, 80–92
Put, 4, 33, 34, 36, 45
Reconsidered, 38
Stated, 4, 33–5, 44, 48
Questions asked, 139, 140
Miscellaneous, 131–46
Quorum, 24, 25
Want of, 74, 79, 161

Repetition, 4
Reports, 141–3
Resolution, 137
Extraordinary, 164
Rescinded, 145, 146
Special, 165
Ruling challenged, 77

Select Committees, 116–30
Special Meetings, 147–51
Business considered at, 149
How convened, 148
Notice of, 149, 150
Special Resolution, 165

Tellers, 63
" The Question is," 9
Time Limit, 95–8

H. A. Shearring and B. C. Christian

TALKS AND HOW TO GIVE THEM
OR SAY WHAT YOU MEAN

This book clearly surveys the barriers between speaker and audience and sets out how they can be overcome. Effective speaking and the essential feeling of contact with a really interested audience can be attained by readers who follow the authors' advice. Their companion volume, *Reports and How to Write Them* (second printing), deals with similar problems in report writing. Indeed the problems come close together when a talk is also to be published, and the two books can well be read together.

Cr. 8vo

Beryl Heitland

HOW TO CONDUCT
A DISCUSSION GROUP

"I have not come across a book like this. It gives them the whole thing in a form which can be easily applied." *From a Youth Organizer and Club Leader*

"A much needed book for the Staff Library of all Secondary and Grammar Schools. I intend to work with the book entirely for my English next year." *From a Secondary Modern School Teacher*

Cr. 8vo

WRITE WHAT YOU MEAN

by R. W. Bell

This book is an aid to writing any type of document normally required for administrative or executive work, whether in private enterprise or the public service. It is a practical book, dealing with a common, everyday problem—how to convey your meaning fully, concisely and effectively.

The author analyses the elements of meaning and shows how they should be dealt with in the various cases—letters, reports, orders, regulations, announcements, minutes, etc. There is a special chapter on documents which may later form the basis of negotiation or dispute.

Cr. 8vo

UNACCUSTOMED AS I AM

by C. Kent Wright

Speaking after dinner is a much neglected art. This little book is intended to help those who are called upon to practise it.

The author, whose earlier anthology, *Nectar in a Nutshell*, will be remembered by many readers, first gives some simple advice about the preparation of after-dinner speeches. In the remaining part of the book, he has collected quotations on fifty different subjects—food, marriage, art, planning, clothes, gastronomy, the atom, politicians, gardening are among the subjects covered.

Cr. 8vo

GEORGE ALLEN & UNWIN LTD